·TESCO· COOKERY· COLLECTION·

BREAD COOKERY
RECIPES AND IDEAS USING BREAD

TESCO

Recipes developed by Kate Moseley
Additional assistance from the Tesco Consumer Kitchens

Published exclusively for Tesco Stores Ltd.
Delamare Road, Cheshunt, Herts EN8 9SL
by Cathay Books, 59 Grosvenor Street, London W1

First published 1986

© Cathay Books 1986

ISBN 0 86178 390 5

Printed in Hong Kong

ACKNOWLEDGEMENTS

The publishers would like to thank the following
who were concerned in the preparation of the book.

Series Art Director Pedro Prà-Lopez
Photographer Chris Crofton
Stylist Barbara Stewart
Food prepared for photography by Sarah Bush
Special editorial help Cathy Dunn

CONTENTS

NOTE

Standard spoon measurements are used in all recipes

1 tablespoon (tbls) = one 15 ml spoon
1 teaspoon (tsp) = one 5 ml spoon
All spoon measures are level

All eggs are sized 3 or 4 (standard) unless otherwise stated.

For all recipes, quantities are given in both metric and imperial measures. Follow either set but not a mixture of both, as they are not interchangeable.

Following the success of the first 12 books we produced in the Tesco Cookery Collection, we are delighted to be adding 8 new titles to this exciting series. As before, it is the close contact we have with our customers and the feedback we have had through our Consumer Advisory Kitchens which has helped us to select these latest titles. Each one focuses on an area in which our customers have shown particular interest and contains practical background information on the chosen subject together with a wide selection of carefully tested recipes, each one illustrated in colour.

Bread Cookery shows you all sorts of interesting ways to use bread. The recipes and colour photographs illustrate that when it comes to versatility, bread is unbeatable. It is also economical and forms part of a healthy diet. There are many varieties of bread, from the humble white farmhouse loaf to delicious nutty wholemeal cobs and rolls. Bread loaves can be hollowed out and filled with a whole range of different fillings; or made into stuffings, coatings, toppings and croûtons. If you need fresh ideas for sandwiches or canapés, turn to pages 50-57, you won't be able to resist them! *Bread Cookery* also provides an informative introduction and a chapter on how to make bread successfully. I very much hope you will enjoy looking through these pages and trying the recipes with your friends and family.

Carey Dennis, chief home economist, Tesco Stores Ltd.

INTRODUCTION

Bread has been a staple food for thousands of years. The first breads were made from a variety of crushed grains and were unleavened – no raising agent was used – so they were more like savoury biscuits than what we now think of as bread.

The Egyptians, around 3000BC, were the first to use yeast in bread making. A few thousand years later the Romans introduced sophisticated bread-making techniques to Britain, including a process for refining white flour. Early bread in Britain was made mostly from rye and barley. Wheat only began to take over in the 18th century.

Now the range of breads available is vast, yet the amount of bread we eat is declining. This is partly because with the variety of foods there are to choose from, bread, with all its versatility, can be neglected. It is also partly because many people have the mistaken impression that bread is fattening, which is not the case. It is the butter or margarine, marmalade or jam that are high in calories. Bread itself fills you up long before it breaks any calorie barriers.

BREAD IN YOUR DIET

All types of bread are nutritious: they provide protein, starchy carbohydrates and fibre and are also low in fat. Wholemeal bread, which provides a bumper package of B vitamins, vitamin E and fibre, is best, but white bread, fortified as it is with calcium and iron, is also valuable. White bread with added bran is available, if you want extra fibre but prefer white bread to wholemeal.

There are all sorts of ways you can use bread besides the familiar sandwiches and toast. The recipes that follow demonstrate how you can make bread an integral part of your everyday meals.

This book shows you how you can use bread; white, brown or wholemeal, as a filling, topping or base for original dishes. You can make croûtons, breadcrumb dumplings, or crusty toppings for soups and casseroles. You can use breadcrumbs as stuffing for meat and vegetables, or to make pâtés, soufflés or burgers go further. You can even use bread in desserts; not just the familiar bread pudding and summer pudding, but many others you may not have thought of. And bread is an ideal ingredient for quick snacks or party titbits.

DIFFERENT TYPES OF FLOUR

Since almost all the bread we eat is made from wheat, the main difference between varieties is the way the flour is milled.

To make white flour the wheat grains are milled and the bran (exterior husk) and wheatgerm (nutritious part of the grain that germinates) are extracted and removed. Sometimes the flour is bleached to make it whiter. Unbleached flour is a creamy colour.

Brown flour differs only from white flour in that it contains a small proportion of bran.

Wholemeal or wholewheat flour is the whole wheat grain, milled – nothing added, nothing taken away.

Stoneground wholemeal flour is simply flour made in the traditional way using grinding stones. It is no more nutritious than any other wholemeal flour.

BREAD TERMS

It is important to clear up some of

the confusing names when referring to types of bread.

White varieties of bread are made from white flour but may also be enriched with egg.

Wheatgerm bread is made either from white or brown flour to which some wheatgerm is added. The most common brand name is Hovis.

Bran-enriched bread is made from either white, brown or wholemeal flour to which extra bran is added.

Malted mixed grain bread is made from either white or brown flour to which malted (germinated and dried) grains, e.g. barley, rye or wheat are added. The most common brand name is Granary.

Wholemeal bread is made from wholemeal flour. The brand name Rustic is used for wholemeal bread made from wholewheat grains that have been crushed or flaked rather than ground.

Fruited bread (or tea bread) is made from any of the flour varieties to which dried fruits and/or sugar and spices are added.

Seeded bread is made from any of the flour varieties to which sesame or maw (poppy-type) seeds are added.

Here are descriptions of some of the bread varieties you may encounter:

Baguette/Baton

A crusty French stick made in the traditional French way. The baguette, longer and thinner than the baton, is available in plain white, Rustic wholemeal and seeded (15) versions. The baton is available in plain white (13), Rustic wholemeal (14), seeded (17), and onion (16) versions.

Bap

Baps are light, soft and are dusted with flour before baking. Available in white (26), bran (30), stoneground wholemeal (32), brown and sesame-seeded versions, plus a special white bun with sesame seeds for burgers (21).

Batch
These loaves are baked packed together on a baking sheet – no tin is used. They are soft and do not have crusts on the sides. Available white, wholemeal and fruited (44).

Bloomer
A plump, crusty loaf with diagonal cuts across the top, available in plain white (6) and also seeded versions.

Cholla
A white bread, enriched with egg, plait- (5) or knot-shaped and seeded. A Jewish speciality.

Cob/Coburg
A round, crusty loaf, sometimes with cuts in the top, made in white (4), malted mixed grain (8) and Rustic wholemeal versions.

Croissant
A crescent-shaped roll, with a light, flaky texture. Made by layering yeast dough with margarine or butter. Uses white flour and comes plain (18a) or seeded (18b).

Crumpet
Made from a batter mixture and baked in a ring on a hot plate or griddle. Crumpets have an open texture produced by the action of yeast, raising agent and heat. They are available in white (35) and bran (34) versions and have to be toasted before eating.

Danish
This is a light, open white bread enriched with a little extra fat and sugar. It is ideal for toasting.

Farmhouse
A wider than average loaf with a floured crust that usually has a deep cut down the centre. Available in white (2) or muesli (38) versions.

Fruited bread
There are many varieties of sweet, fruited bread, such as Hovis tea bread (41), tea cakes (42), fruit buns (43), the fruit Windmill loaf (40) and the muesli farmhouse (38).

Malt loaf
Malt extract and malt flour combined with moist vine fruits and kneaded into a dough with unbleached wheat flour produces this

delicious, sticky loaf (39).

Muffin

This is a famous English speciality which, like a crumpet, is more of a yeast cake than bread. It also should be toasted. Available in white and wholemeal (33) versions.

Pitta bread

Traditional Greek bread made in white (37) and wholemeal (36) versions. It uses little yeast and has a characteristic flat, oval shape. Another Greek speciality is white bread sprinkled with sesame seeds. This loaf has several cross-cuts and splits easily into chunks.

Rolls

Available in many shapes and sizes. You can get crusty bread rolls in white (19), finger rolls in white (25) and brown (29), snack rolls in white (24) and brown (28), malted mixed grain rolls and fruit rolls. For break-fast you can have a wide variety of morning rolls: white (23), brown (27), and continental in plain white (22), seeded (20) and wholemeal (31) versions.

Rye bread

This is made with a mixture of rye and wheat flours, and usually has a sprinkling of caraway seeds (7).

Scones

Scones are risen with bicarbonate of soda rather than yeast, and may have dried fruit added.

Sliced

Pre-sliced bread is made from many different flours: white, brown, brown with extra wheatgerm or bran, wholemeal and stoneground wholemeal. Hi-Fibre white bread is a special bread with added vegetable fibre. Scottish bread is a soft, sliced loaf similar to a large batch loaf.

Soda

The raising agent for this bread is not yeast but bicarbonate of soda. It is round and deeply scored so that it breaks easily into quarters. Available white, brown (11) or fruited.

Tin loaf

Most large loaves are made in tins. The split tin loaf (1) has a deep cut, like the farmhouse, but is a longer and thinner loaf with a firmer top

crust. The Natural (3) is a white loaf made to a special recipe using less refined white flour, less salt than normal and all-vegetable fat. Other tin loaves include a crusty brown (9), rustic wholemeal (12), malted mixed grain and plain wholemeal.

Windmill

A round flat loaf divided into segments characteristic of a 'windmill'. Available white, fruited (40), seeded or brown (10).

KEEPING BREAD

Bread keeps longer if you store it well. Keep bread tins free of crumbs and wipe out with vinegar occasionally to prevent mould. It is better to wrap bread in a clean, dry cloth than in a polythene bag and it is not a good idea to store bread in the refrigerator. The temperature may prevent mould but it makes the bread dry.

Freezing is an ideal way to store bread over long periods. If you are freezing home-baked bread, let it cool first. Wrap the bread closely in a polythene bag or foil and put it in the freezer while fresh. Alternatively, make breadcrumbs from fresh or slightly stale bread and freeze them in a polythene bag.

You needn't waste bread that is slightly stale. Besides using it to make breadcrumbs for coating, it is important to use slightly stale bread for croûtes and croûtons so that they do not soak up too much fat, but go crisp quickly. Fresh breadcrumbs are specified in recipes which need moister bread.

Freeze bread in slices or pieces for greater convenience. You can toast sliced bread from frozen. Otherwise, to thaw bread, unwrap it and leave it at room temperature. A large loaf takes three to four hours to thaw. If you are in a hurry, you can put a whole loaf straight from the freezer (unwrapped) into a medium oven for around half an hour or thaw in the microwave. You can use breadcrumbs straight from the freezer in cooking – just break them up with your fingers.

31 34 41 38 35 39 42 36 37 43 44 33 40

French onion soup

SERVES 4

450 g (1 lb) onions, thinly sliced
25 g (1 oz) butter or margarine
1 tsp vegetable oil
1.2 litres (2 pints) vegetable or
  chicken stock
salt and pepper
2 tbls plain flour
150 ml (¼ pint) water
To garnish
4 slices French baton or baguette
25 g (1 oz) butter or margarine
2 tsp herb or Dijon mustard
50 g (2 oz) Gruyère cheese, grated

Place the onions in a large frying pan with the butter and oil. Cover and cook the onions over gentle heat for 8-10 minutes until soft and transparent. Remove the lid and fry until the onions are golden.

Stir in the stock and season to taste. Replace the lid and simmer for 30 minutes.

Meanwhile, heat the oven to 180°C, 350°F, Gas Mark 4. To prepare the garnish, spread both sides of the bread with butter and one side with mustard. Place the slices, mustard side up, on a baking sheet and sprinkle with cheese.

Bake in the oven for 10-15 minutes until the bread is crisp and the cheese has melted.

Mix the flour and water together. Add to the soup and stir until it comes to the boil. Simmer for a few minutes until the soup is thickened.

Place a slice of bread in individual warmed soup bowls and pour the soup over the top. The slices of French bread could be floated on top of the soup, if preferred.

Tomato soup with chilli croûtons

SERVES 4

25 g (1 oz) vegetable margarine
1 large onion, sliced
1 large carrot, sliced
450 g (1 lb) tomatoes, skinned and
  chopped
600 ml (1 pint) vegetable stock
50 g (2 oz) split lentils
1 bay leaf
pinch of grated nutmeg
salt and pepper
4 tbls natural yoghurt, to garnish
For the croûtons
2 thick slices white bread, crusts
  removed
25 g (1 oz) butter or margarine
1 tbls vegetable oil
good pinch of chilli powder

Melt the vegetable margarine in a large saucepan and fry the onion and carrot for 2-3 minutes.

Add the tomatoes, stock, lentils, bay leaf and nutmeg. Season to taste. Bring to the boil, cover and simmer for 40 minutes.

To make the croûtons, cut the bread into 1 cm (½ inch) cubes. Heat the butter and oil in a small pan and sprinkle in the chilli powder. Add the bread cubes and fry all over until crisp and golden. Drain on absorbent kitchen paper.

Purée the soup in a food processor or blender, then return to the pan. Reheat until it boils.

Ladle the soup into warmed bowls and swirl a little yoghurt into each bowl. Sprinkle with a few croûtons.

● **Above: Tomato soup with chilli croutons; Below: French onion soup**

Quick chicken liver pâté

SERVES 4

50 g (2 oz) butter or margarine
1 onion, chopped
2 garlic cloves, crushed
225 g (8 oz) chicken livers, coarsely
   chopped
100 g (4 oz) button mushrooms,
   chopped
2 tbls sherry
salt and pepper
2 medium slices white or
   wholemeal bread, crusts
   removed
little milk
1 bay leaf, to garnish

Melt the butter in a medium frying pan and fry the onion and garlic over a moderate heat for 2 minutes. Add the chicken livers and mushrooms and stir-fry for 3 minutes. Stir in the sherry and season to taste. Bring to the boil, cover and simmer gently for 15-20 minutes.

Place the bread in a food processor or blender and make breadcrumbs. Add the chicken liver mixture and blend until an almost smooth pâté, adding a little milk if necessary.

Spoon into a serving dish and garnish with the bay leaf. Chill until 10 minutes before serving.

Serving idea: Using a nozzle and piping bag, pipe onto thin slices of

• Above: Quick chicken liver pâté;
Below: The full range of savoury butters
for Hot breads

crisp brown toast or Melba toast.
Garnish with strips of red pepper,
sliced mushrooms and chopped
chives. To make Melba toast, toast
thin slices of white or brown bread
on both sides. Split the slices
through the middle and toast the
uncooked surfaces under a hot grill.
Alternatively, cut stale bread into
very thin slices, place on a baking
sheet and leave them to crisp and
curl in the bottom of a cool oven.
Variation: You can use 50 g (2 oz)
melted butter to seal the surface of
the pâté, if you like.

Hot breads

SERVES 8

*1 crusty white French stick, or
    maw-seeded baguette*

FOR SAVOURY BUTTERS

To 100 g (4 oz) butter, softened, add
one of the following: (***Note:*** Com-
mercially prepared butters are
also available.)

1 Lemon and parsley
rind and 2 tbls juice of 1 lemon
2 tbls chopped fresh parsley

2 Horseradish
2 tbls creamed horseradish

3 Mustard
2 tbls coarse-grained mustard
1 tsp Dijon mustard

4 Ham and pineapple
*50 g (2 oz) cooked ham, finely
    chopped or minced*
*227 g (8 oz) crushed pineapple,
    drained*

5 Spring caper
6 spring onions, chopped
2 tbls capers, chopped

6 Blue cheese
*75 g (3 oz) Roquefort, Stilton or
    Bavarian Blue cheese*

7 Herbs and garlic
2-3 garlic cloves, crushed
2-3 tbls chopped fresh mixed herbs

8 Peppercorn and coriander
1 tsp black peppercorns, crushed
1 tsp green peppercorns, crushed
1 tsp coriander seeds, crushed

Heat the oven to 200°C, 400°F, Gas
Mark 6. Cut the French bread in
1 cm (½ inch) slices almost through
to the base. Spread each slice with the
chosen savoury butter. Wrap in foil.
Cook in the oven for 15 minutes.

Stilton baked mushrooms

SERVES 4

8 slices granary or wheatgerm
  bread
8 medium-sized field or flat
  mushrooms, wiped
65 g (2½ oz) blue cheese butter (see
  page 13)
1 small onion, finely chopped
2 slices cooked ham, finely
  chopped
50 g (2 oz) Stilton cheese, crumbled
  or grated
salt and pepper
1 egg, beaten
little vegetable oil
To garnish
2 tsp chopped fresh chives
2 sprigs of mint

Heat the oven to 190°C, 375°F, Gas
Mark 5. Cut the bread slices into
rounds the same size as the
mushrooms. (Use a pastry cutter or
a teacup for guidance.) Make the
crusts into breadcrumbs.

Remove and chop the stalks from
the mushrooms. Melt 25 g (1 oz) of
the butter and fry the stalks and
onion for 3 minutes until soft.

Add the breadcrumbs and fry for 2
minutes. Remove from the heat and
stir in the ham and cheese. Season.

Add enough egg to bind the mixture together. Brush a little oil all
over the mushrooms and place
them, rounded side down, in a lightly greased baking tin.

Spoon some filling into each
mushroom, pressing it down and
then doming the top slightly.

Cover with lightly oiled foil. Bake
in the oven for 15-20 minutes.

Toast the bread rounds on both
sides and spread with the butter.

Arrange the toast on a warmed
serving platter or individual plates
and place a mushroom on each
round. Sprinkle with chopped
chives, garnish with mint sprigs
and serve immediately.

Scrambled toasties

SERVES 2

45 g (1½ oz) butter or margarine,
  softened
4 slices medium sliced brown or
  white bread, crusts removed
3 eggs
2 tbls milk
50 g (2 oz) cooked ham or salami,
  finely chopped
2 tbls sweetcorn
1 spring onion, trimmed and finely
  chopped
50 g (2 oz) mature Cheddar cheese,
  grated
1 tsp Worcestershire sauce
  (optional)
salt and pepper

Heat the oven to 200°C, 400°F, Gas
Mark 6. Spread half the butter on
both sides of each slice of bread.

Press the bread slices into 4 individual Yorkshire pudding tins,
about 10 cm (4 inches) in diameter,
leaving the corners protruding.
Bake in the oven for 15-20 minutes
until crisp and golden.

Five minutes before the toasts are ready, melt the remaining butter in a small pan over moderate heat. Whisk the eggs and milk in a bowl and pour into the pan. Whisk or stir until the eggs begin to scramble.

Remove from the heat and stir in the ham, sweetcorn and onion. Stir over a low heat for 1-2 minutes and add the cheese and Worcestershire sauce, if using. Season to taste.

Spoon the mixture into the bread cases and serve immediately on warmed plates.

Variation: Any finely chopped meat, like leftover chicken, beef or sausage or crispy bacon, could be added. Use peas, diced pepper or tomato or a handful of frozen mixed vegetables, thawed, instead of sweetcorn. The bread cases can also be made in deep patty tins. The filling can easily be made in a microwave.

Salami pizzas

SERVES 2

2 wholemeal muffins
50 g (2 oz) blue cheese butter (see
page 13)
4 slices salami
4 canned pineapple rings
100 g (4 oz) mature Cheddar
cheese, grated

Heat the grill to moderate. Halve the muffins and toast them lightly on both sides.

Spread each half with the butter. Top with a slice of salami, a pineapple ring and some grated Cheddar cheese.

Place the muffins back under the grill and cook until the cheese melts. Serve hot.

● **Left: Stilton baked mushrooms; Centre: Salami pizzas; Right: Scrambled toasties**

Kofta kebabs in pitta pockets

SERVES 6

6 white or wholemeal pitta breads
For the kebab filling
750 g (1 ½ lb) lean, ground lamb
(see note)
4 spring onions, trimmed and
roughly chopped
2 slices medium sliced white
bread, crusts removed
½ tsp ground cumin
½ tsp ground ginger
½ tsp chilli powder
salt and pepper
1 egg, beaten
For the salad garnish
6 tbls chilli or barbecue relish
6 crisp lettuce leaves, roughly
chopped
3 tomatoes, sliced
6 spring onions, trimmed and
sliced
lemon juice (optional)

To make the kebab filling, mince or blend in a food processor the onions and bread until finely chopped. Mix in the ground lamb.

Add the spices and season to taste. Mix in enough egg to bind the mixture together. Heat the grill to moderate.

Form the mixture into 12 sausage shapes. Cook under the grill for about 10 minutes, turning them until browned all over and cooked through. Keep warm.

Heat the pittas under the grill until puffy. Slit each pitta open to form a pocket and place 2 kebabs into each one. Spoon in some relish and top with the salad ingredients, sprinkling with a little lemon juice, if liked. Serve immediately.

Note: If you are unable to buy ground lamb, the best substitute is 750 g (1½ lb) good quality, lean shoulder lamb, trimmed of all fat and cubed. Mince or blend in a food processor.

Devilled toast snack

SERVES 2-3

225 g (8 oz) frozen chicken livers,
just thawed
1 tbls Worcestershire sauce
few drops of Tabasco sauce
1 tsp mustard powder
1 tsp dried rosemary
1 tsp tomato purée
salt and pepper
65 g (2½ oz) peppercorn and
coriander butter (see page 13)
1 tbls vegetable oil
2-3 × 1 cm (½ inch) thick slices
from a small crusty bloomer
1 rasher back bacon, rinded and
chopped
50 g (2 oz) button mushrooms,
sliced
50 g (2 oz) black or green grapes,
halved and seeded, reserving a
few for garnish

Wash and dry the chicken livers. Cut into 2.5 cm (1 inch) chunks, discarding any stringy bits. Place in a bowl and stir in the Worcestershire and Tabasco sauces, mustard, rosemary and tomato purée. Season to taste. Set aside.

Heat 50 g (2 oz) of the butter with the oil in a medium frying pan. Add the slices of bread and fry on both sides about 5 minutes until golden brown and crisp. Remove the bread from the pan and keep warm. Wipe the pan out with absorbent kitchen paper. Heat the remaining butter in the pan over a moderate heat and fry the bacon for 1 minute. Add the chicken livers and mushrooms and stir-fry for 3-5 minutes until the livers are brown but still pinky in the centre.

Stir in the grapes, taste for seasoning and spoon the mixture on to the bread croûtes. Garnish with the reserved grapes, serve immediately.

Variation: Ordinary butter may be used instead of flavoured butter.

● Above: Kofta kebabs in pitta pockets; Below: Devilled toast snack

Tuna fishcakes

SERVES 4

225 g (8 oz) mashed potato
50 g (2 oz) butter or margarine,
  softened
2 tbls chopped fresh parsley
1 tbls lemon juice
198 g (7 oz) can tuna fish, drained
100 g (4 oz) mature Cheddar
  cheese, grated
salt and pepper
1 egg, beaten
75 g (3 oz) fresh white breadcrumbs
½ tsp grated nutmeg (optional)

Mix the potato, butter, parsley, lemon juice, tuna and cheese in a large bowl. Season to taste. Shape the mixture into 8 balls.

Heat the oven to 200°C, 400°F, Gas Mark 6.

Dip the balls of mixture into the beaten egg, then in the breadcrumbs with the nutmeg added, if using. Coat well, then flatten into round fishcakes.

Place the fishcakes in a lightly greased baking tin and bake in the oven for 40 minutes turning every so often. Remove and then transfer to a warmed plate to serve.

Variation: Use canned salmon or smoked haddock instead of the tuna. You need to cook a good 350 g (12 oz) potatoes to get 225 g (8 oz) mash, or use instant mashed potato for speed.

Note: The fishcakes can be shallow fried in a small amount of oil for 5 minutes on each side, but, if you have time, cooking them in the oven is healthier.

Crusty mushroom baskets

SERVES 4

4 white crusty rolls
For the filling
175 g (6 oz) button mushrooms,
  coarsely chopped
1 tbls lemon juice
40 g (1½ oz) butter or margarine
2 tbls water
40 g (1½ oz) plain flour
150 ml (¼ pint) milk
2 tbls sherry or red wine
1 tbls chopped fresh parsley
salt and pepper

Heat the oven to 160°C, 325°F, Gas Mark 3. Place the rolls on a baking sheet and warm in the oven.

To make the filling, place the mushrooms, lemon juice, 15 g (½ oz) of the butter and the water in a small saucepan. Cover and simmer for 3 minutes. Remove the lid to evaporate most of the liquid.

Melt the remaining butter in a saucepan, add the flour and cook gently, stirring, for 1-2 minutes. Remove from the heat and gradually blend in the milk. Bring to the boil, stirring constantly, then simmer for 2-3 minutes until thickened and smooth.

Whisk in the sherry or wine and parsley and add the mushrooms. Season to taste.

Remove the rolls from the oven and cut a small slice from the top of each one. Push down the insides of the rolls to form a small basket.

Fill the roll with the mushroom mixture and serve immediately.

Variation: Brioche can be used instead of crusty rolls. Try leeks in a cheesy sauce for the filling, cooked in the same way.

● Above left: Crusty mushroom
baskets; Above right: Tuna fishcakes;
Below: Cheesy corn soufflés

Cheesy corn soufflé

SERVES 4

65 g (2½ oz) butter or margarine
50 g (2 oz) fine white or brown
  breadcrumbs
2 tbls chopped fresh parsley
100 g (4 oz) sweetcorn
4 spring onions, trimmed and
  roughly chopped
50 g (2 oz) plain flour
300 ml (½ pint) milk
salt and pepper
3 eggs, size 2, separated
75 g (3 oz) Cheddar cheese, grated
1 egg white

Heat the oven to 190°C, 375°F, Gas Mark 5. Use 15 g (½ oz) of the butter to grease a 1.5 litre (2½ pint) soufflé dish.

Sprinkle in half the breadcrumbs and half the parsley to coat the base and sides of the dish. Place the sweetcorn and spring onions in the dish.

Melt the remaining butter in a saucepan, add the flour and cook gently, stirring, for 1-2 minutes.

Remove from the heat and gradually blend in the milk. Bring to the boil, stirring constantly, then simmer for 2-3 minutes until thickened and smooth. Season to taste. Cool for a few minutes.

Beat in the egg yolks and 50 g (2 oz) of the cheese.

Whisk the 4 egg whites to the soft peak stage in a large bowl. Add 2 tablespoons egg white to the sauce mixture and mix in well, then carefully fold in the rest of the whites.

Pour the mixture into the prepared dish and sprinkle with the remaining cheese, breadcrumbs and parsley.

Bake in the oven for 35-40 minutes until risen and golden brown.

Serving idea: The mixture can be spooned into 6-8 individual ramekins for serving as a starter and cooked for 15-20 minutes in the oven. Serve with a salad.

Florentine spicy mince

SERVES 4

450 g (1 lb) ground lamb (see Note,
    page 16) or beef
1 onion, chopped
1 small green pepper, deseeded
    and chopped
1 green chilli, deseeded and finely
    chopped
salt and pepper
1½ tsp ground cinnamon
1 tsp grated nutmeg
397 g (14 oz) can tomatoes
2 tsp gravy granules or plain flour
450 g (1 lb) fresh spinach, washed
    and chopped
For the topping
6 slices wholemeal baguette
25 g (1 oz) peppercorn and
    coriander butter (see page 13)
100 g (4 oz) mature Cheddar
    cheese, grated

Cook the meat, onion, pepper and chilli in a large pan over moderate heat for 10 minutes. Drain off any excess fat if necessary.

Add seasoning to taste, the spices and tomatoes and cook, stirring occasionally, for 20 minutes. Mix the gravy granules or flour in a little water and stir into the mince. Simmer until thickened, stirring.

Place the spinach in a large pan and cook without water for about 6 minutes until softened. Drain well, pressing out any water.

Heat the grill to moderate. Transfer the mince to a 1.5 litre (2½ pint) deep flameproof dish and spoon the spinach over the top.

To make the topping, spread the bread with the butter and arrange, buttered side up, on top of the spinach. Sprinkle with the cheese, season, and cook under the grill until the cheese melts. Serve hot.

● **Below: Derby topped chicken; Above:
Florentine spicy mince**

Derby topped chicken

SERVES 4

6-8 chicken thighs, skinned
25 g (1 oz) herbs and garlic butter
    (see page 13)
salt and pepper
1 large eating apple, cored and
    grated
150 ml (¼ pint) cider
For the topping
4 rashers streaky bacon, rinded
    and chopped
3 slices thick sliced white bread,
    cubed
4 tbls natural yoghurt

100 g (4 oz) Sage Derby cheese, crumbled

Heat the oven to 190°C, 375°F, Gas Mark 5. Place the chicken in a roasting tin and spread each thigh with a little herbs and garlic butter. Season to taste. Add the apple to the tin and pour the cider around the chicken.

Bake in the oven for 30-40 minutes. Meanwhile make the topping. Spread the bacon pieces and bread cubes on a baking sheet. Bake in the oven above the chicken for 30 minutes, stirring occasionally until the bread crisps and browns.

Transfer the chicken thighs to a warmed ovenproof serving dish. Boil the juices in the roasting tin for 1 minute. Remove from the heat, stir in the yoghurt and half the Sage Derby. Pour the sauce over the chicken and sprinkle with the bacon and bread topping and remaining cheese.

Place in the oven for 5-10 minutes until the cheese starts to melts.

Serving idea: This is quite a rich dish so it needs a crispy vegetable accompaniment, for example, stir-fried leeks, courgettes and cabbage.

Liver burgers

SERVES 4

175 g (6 oz) wholemeal bread
1 onion, coarsely chopped
350 g (12 oz) lamb's liver
1 tsp dried sage
1 tsp dried thyme
2 tsp Worcestershire sauce
1 egg
salt and pepper
little plain flour
2-3 tbls vegetable oil, for frying

Put the bread into a food processor or blender to make coarse crumbs.

Add the remaining ingredients, except the flour and oil, and blend.

With floured hands, divide the mixture into 8 and shape into balls, then flatten to make burgers.

Heat the oil in a large frying pan and fry each burger for 3-4 minutes on each side. Drain on absorbent kitchen paper before serving.

Serving idea: Serve in sesame buns with corn relish and salad.

Wiltshire faggots

MAKES 16, SERVES 6-8

225 g (8 oz) caul fat or a little flour
  and lard (see Note below)
750 g (1½ lb) pigs' liver
350 g (12 oz) belly pork, rinded and
  boned
2 large onions, coarsely chopped
225 g (8 oz) fresh white
  breadcrumbs
1½ tbls dried sage
salt and pepper
For the sauce
300 ml (½ pint) beef stock
2 tbls red wine
1 tbls gravy granules

Soak the caul fat in a bowl of cold water for about 15 minutes.

Mince or place in a food processor in batches, the liver, pork and onions. Stir in the breadcrumbs and sage. Season to taste.

Heat the oven to 190°C, 375°F, Gas Mark 5.

Divide the meat mixture into 16 and form into balls. Wrap them round with caul fat like a parcel.

Place the faggots in a lightly greased roasting tin. Bake in the oven for 45 minutes.

To make the sauce, whisk all the ingredients in a small pan over a moderate heat until the sauce thickens.

Transfer the faggots to a serving dish and pour the sauce over.

Serving idea: These are best served with mashed potatoes, carrots and cabbage.

Variation: To give the faggots an Italian flavour, add 1 tbls dried oregano to the mixture instead of the sage and add chopped fried onion and red pepper and tomato purée to the sauce.

Note: Caul fat keeps the faggots moist and in good shape. It can be bought very cheaply from a good butcher. If you cannot get any, roll the balls of mixture in a little flour, pack them tightly in a roasting tin and brush with melted lard.

This recipe makes a large quantity because it saves time and is a lot easier in the long run to make a good sized batch. The faggots will freeze well in portion or family packs. They can be thawed in the refrigerator and then reheated at 180°C, 350°F, Gas Mark 4 for 20 minutes, thinning the sauce a little if necessary. Or, reheat from frozen in the microwave; 8 faggots will take 6-8 minutes on Full Power.

● **Left: Wiltshire faggots; Right: Liver burgers**

Beef rolls

SERVES 6

*6 thin slices beef topside, weighing
    about 500 g (1 ¼ lb)*
2 tbls horseradish sauce or cream
1 tbls vegetable oil
1 small onion, chopped
2 carrots, chopped
300 ml (½ pint) beef stock
150 ml (¼ pint) red wine
1 tbls tomato puree, optional
For the stuffing
1 tbls vegetable oil
1 medium onion, finely chopped
*3 rashers streaky bacon, rinded
    and chopped*
3 sticks celery, finely chopped
*75 g (3 oz) fresh white or brown
    breadcrumbs*
25 g (1 oz) shredded suet
1 tbls chopped fresh parsley
*1 tsp chopped fresh or ½ tsp dried
    thyme*
salt and pepper

Place the beef slices between 2
sheets of wetted greaseproof paper
and beat lightly with a rolling pin
until wafer thin. Spread some horseradish sauce on each slice.

Heat the oven to 170°C, 325°F,
Gas Mark 3.

To make the stuffing, heat the oil
in a large frying pan and fry the
onion, bacon and celery for 5 minutes. Stir in the remaining stuffing
ingredients. Divide the stuffing between the beef slices and roll them
up, tucking in the ends to make
parcels. Tie with string or cotton or
hold together with cocktail sticks.

Heat the oil in the frying pan and
fry the rolls for 2-3 minutes until
browned all over. Transfer them to a
shallow ovenproof casserole. Add the
onion and carrot to the pan and fry
for 5 minutes over a moderate heat.
Stir in the stock and wine, bring to
the boil and simmer for 5 minutes.
Pour over the rolls in the casserole.

Cover and cook in the oven for 1½
hours or until tender.

Remove the beef rolls from the
casserole and carefully remove the
string or cocktail sticks. Arrange the
rolls on a warmed serving platter
and keep hot.

Blend the sauce until smooth in a
food processor or blender. Reheat in
a small pan, adding a little tomato
purée for flavour, if necessary. Season to taste.

Pour a little sauce over the rolls
and serve the remainder separately.

Serving idea: Serve with duchesse
potatoes and a selection of colourful,
crunchy vegetables.

● **Left: Glamorgan sausages; Right:
Beef rolls**

Glamorgan sausages

MAKES 8, SERVES 4

150 g (5 oz) mature Cheddar or
Caerphilly cheese, grated
175 g (6 oz) fresh white or
wholemeal breadcrumbs
2 tbls finely chopped leek or spring
onion
2 tbls chopped fresh parsley
2 tsp chopped fresh or 1 tsp dried
sage
1 tsp mustard powder
salt and pepper
2 eggs
2 tbls vegetable oil, for frying

Mix the cheese with 100 g (4 oz) of the breadcrumbs, the leek, parsley, sage and mustard. Season to taste. Bind with 1 egg and an egg yolk.

Divide the mixture into 8 and form into 'sausages'. Lightly whisk the egg white with a fork. Dip the 'sausages' in the egg white, then roll them in the remaining bread-crumbs.

Heat the oil in a large frying pan and fry the 'sausages' for 8-10 minutes turning several times over a moderate heat until crisp, lightly browned and heated through.

Serving idea: These 'sausages' can be served with poached eggs, grilled bacon and tomatoes for a supper dish, or with a colourful salad for a snack lunch.

Farmhouse goulash

SERVES 4

3 tbls vegetable oil
750 g (1½ lb) stewing beef or braising steak, trimmed and cut into 2.5 cm (1 inch) cubes
1 onion, chopped
2 tbls paprika
2 tbls plain flour
250 ml (8 fl oz) beef stock
397 g (14 oz) can tomatoes
1 tbls tomato purée
100 g (4 oz) mushrooms, quartered
For the topping
75 g (3 oz) self-raising flour
75 g (3 oz) fresh white or brown breadcrumbs
75 g (3 oz) shredded suet
½ tsp baking powder
2 tsp cumin seeds
6 tbls soured cream or natural yoghurt
3-4 tbls water

Heat the oven to 180°C, 350°F, Gas Mark 4. Heat the oil in a large frying pan and fry the beef for 5 minutes until browned. Transfer the meat into a round casserole.

Add the onion to the frying pan and fry for 3 minutes. Stir in the paprika and flour. Cook for 1 minute.

Add the stock, tomatoes and tomato purée. Bring to the boil, simmer for 2 minutes then pour over the meat. Cover and cook in the oven for 1¼ hours.

To make the topping, mix the flour, breadcrumbs, suet, baking powder and cumin seeds in a bowl. Season to taste. Add the soured cream or yoghurt and enough water to make a soft dough.

Knead the dough on a lightly floured surface and roll out to the same size as the top of the casserole. Cut the dough into quarters.

Stir the mushrooms into the casserole, then place the 4 pieces of dough on the top. Continue cooking, uncovered, in the oven for 35 minutes. Serve hot with vegetables.

Spicy pork roll

SERVES 4-6

750 g-1 kg (1¾-2 lb) piece boned streaky pork, skin scored
salt and pepper
1 tbls vegetable oil
1 tbls salt
For the stuffing
15 g (½ oz) butter or margarine
1 small onion, finely chopped
1 garlic clove, crushed
2 tsp finely chopped fresh root ginger
1 tsp cumin seeds
2 tsp coriander seeds, crushed
1 tsp ground cumin
50 g (2 oz) mushrooms, chopped
50 g (2 oz) fresh white breadcrumbs

Heat the oven to 190°C, 375°F, Gas Mark 5. To make the stuffing, melt the butter in a small pan and fry the onion, garlic, ginger and cumin seeds over moderate heat for 5 minutes until the onion softens.

Add the coriander seeds, ground cumin and mushrooms and fry for 2 minutes. Remove from the heat and stir in the breadcrumbs.

Lay the pork out flat, season to taste and spread the stuffing over.

Carefully roll up from the short end, then tie up with fine string at intervals.

Place the roll in a roasting tin. Coat the skin with the oil, then rub in the salt. Pour water into the roasting tin to a depth of 2.5 cm (1 inch).

Roast in the oven for approximately 1½ hours until crispy on the top. Remove from the oven and leave to stand for 5 minutes. Take off the string and place the pork roll on a warmed serving platter. Cut into slices.

Serving idea: Thicken the juices from the roasting tin if liked and serve separately. Accompany with roast or sauté potatoes and lightly cooked cauliflower or broccoli.

Lemon and parsley plaice

SERVES 4

4 rashers streaky bacon, rinded
4 large plaice fillets, skinned if
    necessary
2 tbls vegetable oil
2 tbls lemon juice
For the stuffing
grated rind of 1 lemon
4 tbls chopped fresh parsley
50 g (2 oz) fresh white breadcrumbs
salt and pepper
50 g (2 oz) butter or margarine,
    melted

Heat the grill to moderate. To make the stuffing, mix all the ingredients together in a small bowl.

Using the blunt edge of a knife, stretch the bacon rashers. Lay each plaice fillet, skinned side up, on top of a bacon rasher.

Divide the stuffing between the fillets and roll up from the wide end. Secure with a wooden cocktail stick. Brush with the oil and lemon juice. Cook under the grill for about 8 minutes, turning once.

Serving idea: This is very quick to prepare so serve with speedy stir-fried vegetables.

● Clockwise from left: Spicy pork roll; Farmhouse goulash; Lemon and parsley plaice

Apricot and almond stuffing

SERVES Sufficient to stuff 2 × 1 kg (2 lb) rolled breast of lamb (3-4 people)

*175 g (6 oz) wheatgerm
  breadcrumbs
100 g (4 oz) dried, no soak apricots,
  finely chopped
6 sticks celery, finely chopped
1 onion, finely chopped
75 g (3 oz) flaked almonds, toasted
2 tbls lemon juice
1 egg, beaten
salt and pepper*

Mix all the ingredients together, binding with the egg.

Serving idea: Use to stuff 2 rolled breast of lamb making any leftovers into stuffing balls. Or serve with duck.

Watercress and mushroom stuffing

SERVES Sufficient to stuff 4 mackerel

*50 g (2 oz) butter or margarine
1 medium onion, finely chopped
100 g (4 oz) mushrooms, chopped
2 slices wholemeal bread, about
  50 g (2 oz), crumbed
1 bunch watercress, washed and
  finely chopped
salt and pepper*

Melt the butter in a large pan and fry the onion for 3 minutes. Add the mushrooms and fry for 1 minute.

Stir in the breadcrumbs and fry gently for 2 minutes. Add the watercress and season to taste. Cook for 1 minute.

Use to stuff the split fish. Cook under a preheated moderate grill for about 6-8 minutes on each side.

Variation: This stuffing will also go well with pork chops. Split up to the bone, fill with stuffing and secure with cocktail sticks before grilling.

Spinach and sausagemeat stuffing

SERVES Sufficient to stuff a 5.5 kg (12 lb) turkey

*15 g (½ oz) butter or margarine
100 g (4 oz) streaky bacon, rinded
  and chopped
225 g (8 oz) celeriac, finely
  chopped
225 g (8 oz) coarse or fine
  sausagemeat
100 g (4 oz) wholemeal
  breadcrumbs
100 g (4 oz) packet frozen chopped
  spinach, thawed and drained
salt and pepper*

Melt the butter in a frying pan and fry the streaky bacon and celeriac for about 5 minutes. Remove from the heat.

Soften the sausagemeat in a large bowl. Add the breadcrumbs, the spinach and bacon and celeriac mixture. Season to taste, then mix together well.

Use to stuff the neck end of a turkey just before cooking.

Devilled stuffing balls

SERVES Sufficient to accompany a roast goose, to serve 6 people, or halve the recipe to serve with game.

*6 rashers streaky bacon, rinded
  and finely chopped
1 small onion, finely chopped
100 g (4 oz) button mushrooms,
  finely chopped
225 g (8 oz) fresh white
  breadcrumbs
12 dried, no soak prunes, chopped
2 tbls chopped fresh parsley
1 tbls Worcestershire sauce
2 tsp mustard powder
2 tsp horseradish sauce or cream
2 tsp tomato purée (optional)
dash of Tabasco sauce
salt and pepper
1 egg, beaten*

● Clockwise from above left: Watercress and mushroom stuffing; Apricot and almond stuffing; Spinach and sausagemeat stuffing; Devilled stuffing balls

Heat oven to 200°C, 400°F. Gas Mark 6.

Fry the bacon in a small pan for 2 minutes. Add the onion and cook for about 3 minutes until softened and browning. Stir in the mushrooms and cook for 1 minute.

Mix the remaining ingredients in a bowl. Add the bacon mixture. Stir.

Shape into 12 balls. Cook in the oven in a greased roasting tin for 20-30 minutes. Serve round the goose, game or pork on a platter.

VEGETABLES

Swiss roulade

SERVES 4

25 g (1 oz) fresh wholemeal
    breadcrumbs
100 g (4 oz) Edam or Gruyère
    cheese, finely grated
50 g (2 oz) low fat soft cheese
4 eggs, separated
150 g (5.29 oz) carton thick-set
    natural yoghurt
salt and pepper
2-3 tbls warm water
1 tbls grated Parmesan cheese
For the filling
175 g (6 oz) low fat curd
    cheese
1-2 tbls skimmed milk
3-4 spring onions, trimmed and
    finely chopped
2 small tomatoes, skinned,
    deseeded and cut in strips
50 g (2 oz) chopped nuts or lean
    smoked ham, cut in strips

Heat the oven to 200°C, 400°F, Gas
Mark 6. Grease and line a 24 ×
34 cm (9½ × 13½ inch) Swiss roll
tin.

Mix together the breadcrumbs
and cheeses, then stir in the egg
yolks and yoghurt. Season to taste
and add enough water to make a
soft consistency.

Whisk the egg whites to the soft
peak stage and carefully fold into the
bread and cheese mixture. Pour the
mixture into the tin.

Bake in the oven for 15-20 minutes or until risen, golden and firm.

Carefully turn the roulade on to a
sheet of greaseproof paper that has
been dusted with Parmesan. Gently
remove the lining paper, easing it
away with the back of a knife. Roll
up the roulade like a Swiss roll with

the paper inside it. Leave to cool.

To make the filling, beat the curd
cheese with the milk until soft and
add the spring onion. Carefully un-
roll the roulade and discard the
paper.

Spread the cheese mixture over
the roulade and spoon over the tomatoes and nuts or ham strips. Roll up
the roulade again.

Serving idea: Serve as a main meal
with salad or in slices as a starter.

Harvest time salad

SERVES 4

2 sticks celery, chopped
2 carrots, grated
2 eating apples, cored and diced
2 plums, stoned and sliced
25 g (1 oz) chopped walnut pieces
salt and pepper
3 tbls orange juice
3 tbls natural yoghurt
2 rashers back bacon, rinded,
    grilled and diced (optional, see
    Variation)
2 tbls chopped fresh chives or
    mixed herbs
2 slices wheatgerm bread, toasted
    and cut into 8 triangles

Mix together the chopped celery,
grated carrots, diced apples, sliced
plums and walnut pieces in a large
salad bowl. Season with salt and
pepper to taste.

Add the orange juice and natural
yoghurt to the bowl and toss the
fruit and vegetables until they are
well coated.

Sprinkle with the chopped bacon
and fresh herbs. Place the toasted
triangles around the edge of the
dish. Serve immediately.

● Above: Swiss roulade; Below: Harvest time salad

Serving idea: This salad makes a delicious accompaniment to cold meats or cheese.

Variation: To serve as a vegetarian meal, add more nuts, for instance chopped hazelnuts or fresh, un-salted almonds. Add cubes of Brie or Cheddar cheese instead of the bacon and add some alfalfa or crunchy bean sprouts.

As an alternative serve this salad as a starter accompanied with some hot bread (see page 13).

31

Brazilian baked aubergines

SERVES 4

2 large aubergines
1 large onion, chopped
½ red pepper, deseeded and
*   chopped*
2 garlic cloves, crushed
1 tbls olive oil
397 g (14 oz) can tomatoes
100 g (4 oz) Brazil nuts, chopped
75 g (3 oz) fresh brown
*   breadcrumbs*
little salt
cayenne or paprika pepper
150 ml (¼ pint) water

Heat the oven to 190°C, 375°F, Gas Mark 5. Halve the aubergines then carefully cut out the flesh, leaving a 1 cm (½ inch) rim around the edge.

Plunge the aubergine shells into boiling water and cook for 1 minute, then plunge them into cold water. Drain well. Place the shells in a lightly greased ovenproof dish.

Chop the aubergine flesh roughly. Place in a large frying pan with the onion, red pepper, garlic and oil. Cook over low heat for 5 minutes.

Add the tomatoes, nuts, breadcrumbs and salt.

Pile the mixture into the aubergine shells, sprinkle with pepper and pour the water around them.

Cover the dish with foil. Bake in the oven for 50 minutes.

Serving idea: Lemon-flavoured brown rice or pasta would go well with the aubergines together with a colourful salad of apple, pineapple, sweetcorn and tomato.

● **Left: Brazilian baked aubergines; Right: Nutty leaf parcels**

Nutty leaf parcels

SERVES 4

12 medium Savoy or spring
  cabbage leaves
300 ml (½ pint) vegetable stock
For the stuffing
1 tbls vegetable oil
1 medium onion, finely chopped
100 g (4 oz) hazelnuts, ground
100 g (4 oz) fresh wholemeal or
  granary breadcrumbs
2 tbls chopped fresh coriander
  leaves
2 tbls chopped fresh parsley
salt and pepper
100 g (4 oz) frozen spinach, thawed
1 egg

Heat the oven to 180°C, 350°F, Gas
Mark 4. Blanch the cabbage leaves
in a saucepan of boiling salted water
for 2 minutes. Refresh in cold water
and drain.

To make the stuffing, heat the oil
in a pan and fry the onion for about
5 minutes. Add the nuts and breadcrumbs and cook for 2 minutes.

Remove from the heat and add the
remaining ingredients. Season to
taste. Divide the mixture in half.

Place 6 of the cabbage leaves on a
flat surface and divide half the stuffing mixture between them. Roll
each leaf up from the base, folding
the sides into the centre.

Pack them tightly, join down-
wards, in a shallow ovenproof dish.
Repeat with the remaining leaves
and stuffing. Pour the stock over the
parcels. Cover and bake in the oven
for 30 minutes.

Serving idea: These parcels can be
served as a main meal. Alternatively,
serve as a starter for 6 people garnished with coriander leaves with
just a little tomato or sweetcorn
relish on the plate.

Vegetable supper with almond dumplings

SERVES 4-6

900 ml (1½ pints) vegetable stock
450 g (1 lb) potatoes, diced
3 carrots, sliced
100 g (4 oz) cauliflower, broken
   into florets
100 g (4 oz) frozen runner beans
50 g (2 oz) frozen peas
25 g (1 oz) butter or margarine
25 g (1 oz) plain flour
1-2 egg yolks
4-6 tbls single cream
salt and pepper
For the dumplings
2 egg whites
100 g (4 oz) wholemeal
   breadcrumbs
50 g (2 oz) ground almonds
2 tsp grated lemon rind
1 tsp ground coriander (optional)
vegetable oil, for frying
50 g (2 oz) flaked almonds,
   toasted, to garnish

To make the dumplings, whisk the egg whites in a bowl until fairly stiff. Sprinkle in the breadcrumbs, the almonds, lemon rind and coriander, if using.

Heat a little oil in a large frying pan and add teaspoons of mixture or form the mixture lightly into about 16 balls. Fry the dumplings for 2-3 minutes until brown all over. Remove from the pan and set aside.

Put the stock, potatoes and carrots into a saucepan. Bring to the boil, cover and simmer for 5 minutes.

Add the cauliflower, beans and peas and bring back to the boil for 4 minutes or until the vegetables are just tender.

Drain the stock into a bowl or jug and set the vegetables aside.

Melt the butter in the pan, add the flour and cook gently, stirring, for 1-2 minutes over moderate heat. Remove from the heat and gradually blend in the stock. Return to the heat and bring to the boil, stirring

constantly, then simmer for about 2-3 minutes until smooth.

Blend the egg yolks and cream together in a small bowl and add 2 tablespoons of the hot stock, then slowly whisk the mixture into the pan over a low heat.

Return the vegetables and almond dumplings. Season to taste and heat through without boiling to prevent curdling.

Serve in individual warmed bowls, sprinkled with flaked almonds.

Serving idea: This is best eaten with a spoon and fork and thick slices of brown bread.

● Left: Vegetable supper with almond dumplings; Right: Courgette and leek bread bake

Courgette and leek bread bake

SERVES 4

15 g (½ oz) butter or margarine
1 tbls water
225 g (8 oz) courgettes, sliced
225 g (8 oz) leeks, sliced
175 g (6 oz) wholemeal bread,
* cubed*
450 ml (¾ pint) milk
2 eggs
175 g (6 oz) mature Cheddar
* cheese, grated*
1 tsp mustard powder
½ tsp dried sage or rosemary
salt and pepper
½ tsp paprika

Heat the oven to 190°C, 375°F, Gas Mark 5. Melt the butter in the water in a large frying pan, add the courgettes and leeks, cover and cook for 3 minutes until the vegetables are tender, but still crunchy. Drain.

Soak the bread in the milk for about 5 minutes until soft. Beat in the eggs, cheese, mustard, and sage or rosemary. Season to taste.

Spoon a third of the bread mixture into a 1.5 litre (2½ pint) ovenproof dish.

Spread half the vegetable mixture on top. Repeat the layers of bread and vegetables, finishing with bread mixture.

Sprinkle with paprika. Bake in the oven for 35 minutes.

Variation: Spring onions, mushrooms or sweetcorn could be used instead of, or as well as, the courgettes and leeks.

Pork peperonata en croûte

SERVES 6

*2 pork fillets, weighing about 700 g
(1½ lb), trimmed
65 g (2½ oz) herbs and garlic butter
(see page 13)
1 onion, chopped
1 red pepper, deseeded and
chopped
1 green or yellow pepper, deseeded
and chopped
397 g (14 oz) can tomatoes,
drained, juice reserved
½ tsp dried oregano
salt and pepper
1 tbls olive oil
6 thick slices of crusty bloomer*

Heat the oven to 180°C, 350°F, Gas Mark 4. If the pork fillets are not already slit in half, prepare by cutting lengthways almost through so that they can be opened out flat. Place both fillets between 2 sheets of wetted greaseproof paper and beat out with a rolling pin to flatten them.

Melt 15 g (½ oz) of the butter in a small pan and fry the onion for 2 minutes. Add the peppers and cook for a further 2 minutes.

Remove from the heat and stir in the tomatoes. Add the oregano and season to taste. Leave to cool.

Spread half the peperonata mixture down the centre of one pork fillet. Place the other fillet on the top, tucking in the sides round the stuffing to enclose it completely. Tie the roll with string.

Heat the olive oil and a little more of the butter in a large flameproof casserole and brown the meat.

Add the remaining peperonata mixture and pour the tomato juice over. Cover and cook in the oven for 1 hour. Remove lid and cook for 30 minutes more to reduce the sauce.

Twenty minutes before the end of cooking time, spread the remaining butter on both sides of the slices of bread. Place on a baking sheet. Bake in the oven for 10-15 minutes until the bread is crisp.

Carefully remove the string and place the meat on a serving plate. Spoon the peperonata mixture on top. Garnish with the garlic croûtes.

Serve the meat in slices on the garlic croûtes.

Serving idea: Serve with pasta noodles and vegetables.

Chicken Cordon Bleu

SERVES 4

4 boned chicken breasts, skinned,
weighing about 700 g (1½ lb)
50 g (2 oz) Gruyère cheese, cut into
4 slices
2 slices cooked ham, halved
1 egg, beaten
75 g (3 oz) fine white breadcrumbs,
dried or toasted
vegetable oil for brushing
To garnish
4 lemon wedges
4 sprigs parsley

Heat the oven to 190°C, 375°F, Gas
Mark 5. Open the chicken breasts
out and place them, 2 at a time,
between 2 sheets of wetted greaseproof paper. Beat lightly with a
rolling pin until thin.

Place a piece of cheese on each
chicken breast. Cover with a piece of
ham. Then roll the breasts up, tucking the sides in to enclose the cheese
and ham. Secure with wooden cocktail sticks. Chill in the refrigerator
for about 30 minutes.

Dip the chicken in beaten egg,
then coat evenly in the breadcrumbs. Chill for another 10 minutes. Place in a lightly greased ovenproof dish. Brush with the oil.

Cook in the oven for 35 minutes
until golden brown. Remove from
the oven. Take out the cocktail
sticks. Serve the chicken garnished
with the lemon wedges and parsley.

Variation: Brush the chicken with a
little melted lemon and parsley butter (see page 13) before cooking.

• Left: Pork peperonata en croûte; Right: Chicken Cordon Bleu

---

Goujons with cocktail sauce

SERVES 4

4 large fillets of sole or plaice,
  skinned
2-3 tbls seasoned flour
2 tsp olive oil
1 egg, beaten
75 g (3 oz) fresh white breadcrumbs
vegetable oil, for deep frying
For the sauce
5 tbls mayonnaise
2 tbls natural yoghurt
1 tsp lemon juice
1 tsp horseradish cream
2 tsp tomato ketchup
dash of Worcestershire sauce
dash of Tabasco sauce (optional)
To garnish
1 lemon, cut into 4 wedges
sprig of parsley

Rinse the fish fillets and dry them on absorbent kitchen paper. Slice each fillet in half at an angle, then cut each piece lengthways into 3 narrow strips. Coat the strips of fish in seasoned flour, shaking off any excess.

Add the olive oil to the beaten egg and dip the fish strips into this mixture, then roll them in the breadcrumbs. Chill in the refrigerator for about 15 minutes.

Meanwhile, make the sauce. Whisk the mayonnaise and yoghurt together in a small bowl. Whisk in the remaining ingredients and pour the sauce into a small serving bowl. Chill in the refrigerator while cooking the fish.

Heat the oil in a large pan until a small cube of bread dropped into it takes 20-30 seconds to brown. Fry the goujons, a few at a time, for about 2-3 minutes until crisp and golden brown. Drain well on absorbent kitchen paper.

Arrange the goujons on a warmed serving plate. Garnish with lemon wedges and parsley. Serve the sauce separately.

Serving idea: Crusty bread and a tomato and cucumber salad could be served with the goujons.

Variations: Make a tartare sauce instead by adding chopped boiled egg, capers and gherkins instead of the tomato, Worcestershire and Tabasco sauces. Try a mild curried sauce or a mustard or pepper sauce for a change, too.

Veal l'ardennaise

This is a simple but easily prepared dish, ideal for entertaining as there is no last minute cooking or garnishing to be done.

SERVES 6

6 escalopes of veal weighing about
  100 g (4 oz) each
For the marinade
4 tbls lemon juice
16 juniper berries or a dash of gin
2 tsp dried marjoram or thyme
salt and pepper
For the topping
50 g (2 oz) butter or margarine
1 onion, chopped
2 medium carrots, sliced
120 ml (4 fl oz) white wine
120 ml (4 fl oz) water
50 g (2 oz) cooked ham, chopped
100 g (4 oz) mixed brown and
  white breadcrumbs
3 tbls chopped fresh parsley

Place the veal in a shallow dish and pour over the lemon juice. Crush the juniper berries with the marjoram or thyme. Sprinkle over the meat and season to taste. Leave to marinate for about 2 hours, turning the meat occasionally.

Heat the oven to 150°C, 300°F, Gas Mark 2.

Melt the butter in a large frying pan and fry the onion and carrot over gentle heat for about 5 minutes. Add the veal pieces and brown all over. Transfer the ingredients to

● Left: Veal l'ardennaise; Right: Goujons served with a spoonful of cocktail sauce

a shallow ovenproof dish.

Add the white wine to the frying pan, bring to the boil and reduce it by half, then add the water. Pour over the meat and vegetables.

Scatter the ham, breadcrumbs and parsley on top. Dot with a little extra butter. Bake in the oven for 30-40 minutes until tender.

Serving idea: Keep the accompaniments as simple as possible – new potatoes, mange tout peas or French beans.

Variation: Venison steaks can be used instead of the veal and cooked tongue or cervelat instead of the ham. Cook the venison for 1-1½ hours.

39

Gefilte fish provençal

SERVES 6

450 g (1 lb) haddock fillets
225 g (8 oz) cod fillets
1 small onion, quartered
1 egg
2 tbls sunflower oil
salt and pepper
8 tbls fresh brown or white
  breadcrumbs
For the sauce
1 tbls sunflower oil
1 onion, finely chopped
1 green pepper, deseeded and
  thinly sliced
397 g (14 oz) can chopped tomatoes
1 tsp sugar
salt and pepper

Heat the oven to 150°C, 300°F, Gas Mark 2.

Lightly mix the fish and onion in a food processor or blender. Add the egg, oil and breadcrumbs. Season to taste and blend until the ingredients are well mixed.

Form the fish mixture into golf ball sized balls and arrange these carefully on the base of a large ovenproof dish.

To make the sauce, heat the oil in a pan and fry the onion and pepper for 3 minutes until beginning to soften and turn transparent. Add the tomatoes and sugar. Season to taste with salt and pepper. Simmer for 5 minutes.

Pour the sauce over the fish balls. Cover the dish with foil. Bake in the

40

• Above: Quick coquilles; Below: Gefilte fish provençal

Quick coquilles

SERVES 4

70 g (2.4 oz) packet instant mashed potato
For the filling
225 g (8 oz) cooked whiting, skinned, boned and flaked
50 g (2 oz) scallops quartered
50 g (2 oz) peeled prawns
2 spring onions, trimmed and chopped
2 tbls chopped fresh parsley
6 tbls fresh white breadcrumbs
1 tomato, skinned, deseeded and chopped
5 tbls natural yoghurt
2 tsp tartare sauce
salt and pepper
To garnish
4 unpeeled or 8 peeled prawns
4 large sprigs parsley

Heat the oven to 200°C, 400°F, Gas Mark 6. Make up the potato according to the directions on the packet. Leave to cool slightly.

Spoon the potato into a piping bag fitted with a large star nozzle and pipe a border round the edge of 4 lightly greased scallop shells or small ovenproof dishes. Place on a baking sheet.

Mix all the filling ingredients together well and spoon into the shells or dishes.

Bake in the oven for 12-15 minutes until heated through and the potato is golden. Garnish with the prawns and the 4 large sprigs of parsley.

Serving idea: This dish can be served as a starter or a quick supper dish.

Variation: Use any white fish and add mussels if you like. Frozen fish and shellfish products are very good; do thaw and drain them well before adding to the filling. Add some capers or chopped anchovy fillets for extra interest.

oven for 1½ hours, spooning the sauce over the fish occasionally to keep them moist.

Transfer to a serving dish and serve hot or cold.

Serving idea: Make a batch of Gefilte fish and freeze them in the sauce in 1 or 2 portion packs. They do not take long to thaw: gently reheat in a pan. Alternatively, reheat very quickly from frozen in a microwave.

Variation: Replace the green pepper with a red or yellow pepper.

Red fruits crumble

SERVES 6

*700 g (1½ lb) mixture of red fruits,
e.g. raspberries, redcurrants,
blackcurrants, red or black
cherries, stoned, loganberries,
fresh, canned or thawed if frozen
grated rind and juice of ½ lemon
2 tbls demerara sugar*
For the topping
*175 g (6 oz) fresh granary
breadcrumbs
100 g (4 oz) ground almonds or
hazelnuts
75 g (3 oz) demerara or soft brown
sugar
75 g (3 oz) butter or margarine
25 g (1 oz) flaked almonds
2 tsp coriander seeds, crushed or
1 tsp ground coriander*

Heat the oven to 200°C, 400°F, Gas
Mark 6. Place the fruit in an ovenproof dish. Add the lemon rind, juice
and sugar.

To make the topping, mix the
breadcrumbs, ground almonds or
hazelnuts and demerara or soft
brown sugar together. Rub in the
butter until evenly distributed.
Spoon the crumble over the fruit.
Scatter the flaked almonds and
coriander seeds or ground coriander
on top.

Bake the crumble in the oven for
15 minutes, then reduce the oven
temperature to 180°C, 350°F, Gas
Mark 4 and continue cooking for
about 10 minutes until the top is
browned and the fruit is bubbling.

• Left: Golden syrup tart; Right: Red
fruits crumble

Serving idea: Serve with a mixture
of fresh cream and natural yoghurt.
Soured cream is a delicious alternative to this mixture.

Variation: This topping is also excellent over a mixture of autumn fruits
such as apples, pears, apricots and
plums, but these will need light
cooking first before the topping is
added. Do not be afraid to mix fresh,
frozen and canned fruits to obtain a
colourful combination.

If you don't have any coriander
available, add 1 tsp cinnamon powder or 6 pieces chopped crystallised
ginger to the topping ingredients.

Golden syrup tart

SERVES 4-6

For the pastry
75 g (3 oz) plain flour
75 g (3 oz) wholemeal self-raising
 flour
pinch of salt
40 g (1½ oz) butter or block
 margarine
40 g (1½ oz) lard
1-2 tbls cold water
1 tbls milk
For the filling
8 tbls golden syrup, warmed
100 g (4 oz) coarse brown or white
 breadcrumbs
grated rind and juice of 1 lemon
50 g (2 oz) ginger nut cookies,
 coarsely crushed

Heat the oven to 180°C, 350°F, Gas
Mark 4. To make the pastry, mix the
flours and salt in a large bowl. Rub
in the fats until the mixture looks
like breadcrumbs. Bind together
with the cold water.

Roll out the pastry on a floured
surface and use to line a 20 cm (8
inch) flan dish or flan ring. Reserve
the trimmings. Place in refrigerator
to rest for 30 minutes.

Mix the golden syrup, breadcrumbs, lemon rind and juice together. Spoon the mixture into the
flan case then sprinkle the crushed
cookies on top.

Roll the reserved trimmings, cut
into 6 mm (¼ inch) wide strips and
make a lattice pattern on top. Brush
with milk.

Bake in the oven for 30 minutes.
Serve hot or cold.

Variation: Use double quantity of
breadcrumbs instead of adding the
cookies or add toasted wheatflakes.

French sandwich pudding

SERVES 4-6

600 ml (1 pint) milk
142 ml (5 fl oz) carton whipping
  cream
7.5 cm (3 inch) cinnamon stick
4 eggs
75 g (3 oz) caster sugar
16 slices French baton or baguette,
  about 1 cm (½ inch) thick
50 g (2 oz) butter or margarine
4 tbls raspberry jam
1 tsp ground cinnamon
For the sauce
225 g (8 oz) raspberries, thawed if
  frozen
1 tsp arrowroot or cornflour
1 tbls lemon juice
icing sugar to taste

Heat the oven to 190°C, 375°F, Gas Mark 5. Gently heat the milk, cream and cinnamon stick in a saucepan until just bubbling.

Beat the eggs and sugar together. Remove the cinnamon stick and pour the milk and cream into the eggs.

Spread one side of each slice of bread with the butter and make 8 sandwiches with the jam.

Arrange them in a lightly greased 1.2 litre (2 pint) shallow ovenproof dish and spread butter on top of the sandwiches.

Pour the custard mixture over and sprinkle with the cinnamon.

Place the dish in a roasting tin and pour in boiling water to come two-thirds of the way up the sides of the dish.

Bake in the oven for 40 minutes until the custard is set. Remove the dish from the roasting tin.

Meanwhile make the sauce. Mash, then sieve the raspberries into a saucepan. Stir in the arrowroot and lemon juice, bring to the boil and stir until the sauce thickens. Sweeten with a small amount of icing sugar if necessary.

Serve this pudding warm with the sauce separately.

Variation: This is a sophisticated version of bread and butter pudding. Omit the cream and cut the eggs down to 3 for a less rich pudding. Instead of raspberry jam, make the sandwiches with marmalade and serve with an orange or marmalade sauce.

Spicy bread pudding

SERVES 4

225 g (8 oz) white bread, crust
  removed
300 ml (½ pint) milk
grated rind of 1 lemon
grated rind of 1 orange
50 g (2 oz) butter or margarine,
  melted
75 g (3 oz) soft dark brown sugar
2 tsp ground mixed spice
175 g (6 oz) mixed dried fruit
grated nutmeg

Break the bread into small pieces in a large bowl. Pour over the milk and leave the bread to soak for 30 minutes.

Heat the oven to 180°C, 350°F, Gas Mark 4.

Add all the remaining ingredients, except the nutmeg, to the milk and bread mixture. Stir well, breaking up any lumps of bread.

Spread the mixture in a lightly greased 1.5 litre (2½ pint) deep, ovenproof dish. Sprinkle generously with nutmeg. Bake in the oven for 1¼ hours until golden brown. Serve hot or cold in thick wedges.

Serving idea: If serving hot, accompany with custard or cream.

● Clockwise from left: Apple charlotte; French sandwich pudding; Spicy bread pudding

Apple Charlotte

SERVES 4

3 large cooking apples, peeled,
 cored and chopped
1 tbls lemon juice
65 g (2½ oz) butter or margarine
3 tbls apricot jam or marmalade
2 tbls demerara sugar
10-11 slices white or brown sliced
 bread, preferably 2 days old,
 crusts removed

Place the apple, lemon juice and 15 g (½ oz) of the butter in a small pan over a low heat. Cover and cook to a purée, stirring occasionally.

Add the jam or marmalade and sweeten to taste. Bring the purée to the boil for 5 minutes to reduce until very thick. Set aside to cool slightly.

Heat the oven to 200°C, 400°F, Gas Mark 6.

Melt the remaining 50 g (2 oz) butter and cut the slices of bread in half lengthways.

Brush 14 strips on one side with melted butter. Stand the strips slightly overlapping round a 1.3 litre (2¼ pint) soufflé dish or straight sided ovenproof dish, buttered side to the dish, with the tops coming higher than the top of the dish.

Cut the remaining strips into triangles. Brush one side with butter and arrange half of the triangles, overlapping and buttered side down, on the base of the dish.

Spoon the apple purée into the bread case, smoothing the top. Add the remaining bread triangles to cover the top.

Trim the edge strips down to the level of the top, using scissors.

Bake in the oven for 35 minutes until the bread case is crisp and golden brown.

Leave to stand for 15-20 minutes, then turn out the Charlotte on a warmed serving plate or leave in the dish.

Cinnamon toffee pudding

SERVES 4

150 ml (¼ pint) milk
1 egg, beaten
1½ tsp ground cinnamon
4 slices Greek-style sesame bread,
* or bloomer with sesame seeds,*
* cut into 2.5 cm (1 inch) thick*
* slices, cut in half*
50 g (2 oz) butter or margarine
2 tbls soft brown sugar
4 tbls golden syrup
1 tbls sesame seeds (optional)

Beat the milk, egg and cinnamon together in a small bowl. Dip in the pieces of bread.

Place the butter, sugar, syrup and sesame seeds, if using, in a large frying pan. Heat gently until the mixture begins to froth, then add all the dipped bread pieces at once. Cook for 1-2 minutes on one side, then turn them over to brown on the other side. When they are beginning to get crispy, arrange on a warmed serving plate and pour any remaining toffee mixture over.

Serving idea: Serve natural yoghurt with this sweet dessert, flavoured with ground cinnamon.

● From left: Chocolate surprise; Cinnamon toffee pudding; Danish apple cake

Chocolate surprise

SERVES 4

50 g (2 oz) plain chocolate
75 g (3 oz) butter or margarine
3 eggs
100 g (4 oz) caster sugar
½ tsp vanilla essence
300 ml (½ pint) milk
100 g (4 oz) fresh breadcrumbs
icing sugar, for dusting

Heat the oven to 180°C, 350°F, Gas Mark 4. Melt the chocolate and butter in a small bowl over a pan of hot water. Cool slightly.

Separate 2 of the eggs and gradually add the 2 yolks and the third egg to the chocolate mixture. Then stir in the sugar, vanilla, milk and breadcrumbs.

Whisk the egg whites to soft peak stage and carefully whisk or fold into the chocolate mixture.

Pour the mixture into a 1.75 litre (3 pint) soufflé dish. Place the dish in a roasting tin and pour in boiling water to come halfway up.

Bake in the oven for 50 minutes. Serve the pudding lightly dusted with icing sugar.

Serving idea: Offer cream with this mouth-watering dessert.

Danish apple cake

SERVES 4

1 kg (2 lb) cooking apples, peeled,
  cored and sliced
100 g (4 oz) demerara sugar
3 tsp grated orange rind
100 g (4 oz) butter or margarine
250 g (9 oz) fresh white
  breadcrumbs or grated
  pumpernickel bread
2 tsp ground cinnamon
For the topping
142 ml (5 fl oz) carton double cream
150 g (5.29 oz) carton natural
  yoghurt
15 g (½ oz) plain chocolate, grated

Heat the oven to 200°C, 400°F, Gas Mark 6. Place the apples and half the sugar in a large heavy saucepan. Cover and cook over a low heat until the fruit is soft and pulpy. Stir in the grated orange rind.

Melt the butter in a large frying pan and add the breadcrumbs and remaining sugar with the cinnamon. Stir over a moderate heat for 15-20 minutes until crisp.

Layer a third of the crumbs in the base of a 450 g (1 lb) loaf tin and cover with half the fruit. Repeat these 2 layers, then finish with a layer of breadcrumbs.

Bake in the oven for 20 minutes. Leave to cool. Cover with cling film or foil and chill, overnight.

To serve the pudding, turn out on to a serving plate. Whip the cream until fairly stiff, add the yoghurt and whip until it forms soft peaks.

Pipe or swirl some of the mixture over the top of the dessert and sprinkle with the chocolate. Serve the remaining cream separately.

Austrian nut pudding

SERVES 4-6

50 g (2 oz) butter or margarine,
softened
50 g (2 oz) caster sugar
3 eggs, separated
1 tbls water
1 soft white bap, crumbed
100 g (4 oz) hazelnuts, toasted and
finely ground
For the sauce
410 g (15 oz) can apricot halves,
drained, juice reserved
1 tsp lemon juice
To decorate
2 tbls hazelnuts, toasted and
chopped
2 tbls icing sugar

Butter and sugar a 600 ml (1 pint) pudding basin, using a little of the measured butter and sugar.

Cream the butter and sugar in a bowl until light and fluffy. Add the egg yolks and water and beat again until light. Mix in all of the crumbs and the nuts.

Whisk the egg whites to soft peak stage and lightly whisk into the nut mixture using a balloon whisk. Spoon into the prepared basin, cover with a double layer of pleated greaseproof paper and a piece of pleated foil. (The pudding will rise about 1 cm/½ inch so if you think it unnecessary you can omit to pleat the covering paper.) Tie with string.

Steam the pudding in a steamer or large pan of boiling water for 1½ hours, topping up with boiling water as necessary.

When cooked, turn out the pudding on to a warmed serving plate.

To make the sauce, purée the apricots with the lemon juice in a food processor or blender, place in a small pan and warm through.

Pour some sauce round the base of the pudding. Sprinkle the top with chopped hazelnuts and sifted icing sugar. Serve the remaining sauce separately.

Tropical fruit and nut pudding

This pudding is a variation on the classic English plum or Christmas pudding. Cook it in a pressure cooker to save time and fuel. Alternatively, steam it in a pan or steamer. The pudding can be stored, after cooking, with fresh greaseproof paper and foil on, for 3 months. Reheat by pressure cooking for 30 minutes or steaming for 2 hours.

SERVES 4-6

450 g (1 lb) tropical fruit and nut
mix (including pieces of banana,
pineapple and coconut)
100 g (4 oz) stoned raisins or
sultanas
grated rind and juice of 1 orange

grated rind of 1 lemon
175 g (6 oz) fresh breadcrumbs
1 tsp grated nutmeg
1 tsp ground cinnamon
50 g (2 oz) demerara sugar
2 eggs
2 tbls rum or sherry
85 ml (3 fl oz) milk
100 g (4 oz) butter or margarine,
   melted

Roughly chop any large pieces of nut in the mix. Place the fruit and nut mix, extra fruit, citrus rind and juice, breadcrumbs, spices and sugar in a large bowl.

Beat the eggs with the rum or sherry and milk. Add to the fruit mixture with the butter. Mix well.

Spoon into a lightly greased 1.5 litre (2½ pint) pudding basin and cover with a double layer of pleated greaseproof paper and a layer of pleated foil.

Steam the pudding with 2 litres (3½ pints) water in a pressure cooker for 30 minutes before putting the 15 lb weights on and pressure cooking for 3 hours. Reduce the pressure slowly. Alternatively cook the pudding in a steamer or large pan of boiling water for 6 hours making sure to top up the water at intervals.

Turn out and serve hot.

Serving idea: Accompany with cream, or with rum or brandy butter if serving as an alternative to Christmas pudding.

● **Left: Austrian nut pudding; Right: Tropical fruit and nut pudding**

SANDWICHES

German mustard salami

MAKES 4 ROUNDS

8 slices white crusty bloomer
For the filling
100 g (4 oz) butter or margarine,
    softened
2 tsp German mustard
100 g (4 oz) German peppered
    salami or smoked ham, chopped
1 tbls chopped fresh chives
8 tbls sauerkraut

Mix the butter and mustard well. Add the salami or ham and the chives.

Spread the mixture over 4 slices of the bread and spoon the sauerkraut over. Place the remaining bread slices on top.

Variation: Use any cooked ham and top with coleslaw.

Banana crunch

MAKES 4 ROUNDS

8 medium slices Greek sesame
    bread or sesame seeded batch
For the filling
1 large ripe banana
2 tsp lemon juice
5 tbls crunchy breakfast cereal
1 tbls honey
1 tbls natural yoghurt

Chop the banana and place in a bowl. Add the lemon juice, cereal, honey and yoghurt.

Spoon the mixture on 4 slices of the bread. Top with the remaining bread slices. Cut the sandwiches in half to serve.

Tuna Waldorf

MAKES 6 ROUNDS

10 slices rye bread or pumpernickel
1 head of chicory, chopped
For the filling
198 g (7 oz) can tuna fish in brine,
*   drained and flaked*
1 eating apple, cored and diced
2 tbls chopped walnuts
1 tbls raisins
1 tbls lemon juice
1 tbls honey
4 tbls mayonnaise or natural
*   yoghurt*

Mix the filling ingredients together. Spread the mixture on 5 slices of the rye bread or pumpernickel.

Top with chicory and the remaining bread or pumpernickel slices. Cut into quarters to serve.

Variation: Use canned salmon instead of tuna.

BLT

SERVES 4

65 g (2½ oz) peppercorn and
*   coriander butter (see page 13)*
8 medium slices granary/malted
*   mixed grain cob*
4 crispy lettuce leaves,
*   shredded*
4 tbls mayonnaise
8 rashers back bacon, rinded,
*   grilled and cut into strips*
2 tomatoes, sliced

Spread the butter on the bread. Arrange the lettuce on the top and spoon over the mayonnaise.

Place the bacon over. Halve the tomato slices and place on top. Top with the remaining bread slices and cut in half to serve.

Variation: Use 2 breakfast baps instead of the granary bread slices. Split them and butter the halves.

• From left: German mustard ham; Banana crunch; Tuna Waldorf; BLT

TOASTED SANDWICHES

The recipes for these sandwiches suggest using a toasted sandwich maker. If you do not have a sandwich maker, make them under the grill as follows. Toast all the bread on one side only. Cover half the slices with filling (on the untoasted side) and warm through under the grill. Top with the remaining slices (toasted side up).

Croque monsieur

SERVES 2

40 g (1½ oz) butter or margarine
4 slices medium sliced white or
    brown bread
2 slices cooked ham
1 tsp Dijon mustard
2 slices processed cheese

Heat the sandwich maker. Butter one side of each slide of bread. Place 2 slices of bread, buttered side down, on top of the preheated cooking plate.

Place a slice of ham on top, spread with mustard and top with the cheese and remaining bread slices, buttered side up.

Close lid and toast for 3 minutes.

Variation: Add pickle, pineapple or sliced tomato or substitute the ham or cheese for 4 tbls baked beans.

Scotch woodcock

SERVES 2

4 slices wheatgerm bread
For the filling
40 g (1½ oz) can anchovies in olive
    oil, drained and soaked in milk
    for 1 hour and then washed
65 g (2½ oz) pepper butter (see
    page 13)
2 eggs, beaten
2 tbls single cream or milk

Drain the anchovies and mash all but 4 of them with 50 g (2 oz) of the butter. Spread this on one side of each slice of bread. Halve the remaining anchovies lengthways.

Melt the remaining butter in a pan and add the eggs and cream or milk. Stir over low heat until the eggs are scrambled. Do not let the mixture boil or it may curdle. Heat the sandwich maker.

Place 2 slices of bread, buttered side down, on top of the preheated cooking plate.

Spread each slice with filling and arrange the remaining anchovy fillets on top in a lattice pattern. Cover with the remaining bread slices, buttered side up.

Close lid and toast for 3 minutes.

Cox's cheese toastie

SERVES 2

4 slices wheatgerm bread
40 g (1½ oz) butter or margarine,
    softened
For the filling
1 Cox's apple
1 tbls lemon juice
75 g (3 oz) mature Cheddar cheese,
    or Gouda, grated
1 tbls chopped walnuts
½ tsp Worcestershire sauce
pepper

Quarter and core the apple. Cut 2 quarters into slices and toss them in the lemon juice.

Grate the remaining apple quarters into a bowl, then add the cheese, nuts, Worcestershire sauce and some pepper.

Heat the sandwich maker. Butter one side of each slice of bread. Place 2 slices, buttered side down, on top of the preheated cooking plate.

Spread the cheese mixture over and arrange the apple slices on top. Cover with the remaining bread slices, buttered side up.

Close lid and toast for 3 minutes.

Samosa toast

SERVES 2

4 slices medium sliced white or
  brown bread
50 g (2 oz) butter or margarine
For the filling
1 small onion, finely chopped
1 garlic clove, crushed
1 small dried chilli, chopped
½ tsp chilli powder
75 g (3 oz) minced beef
2 tomatoes, skinned and chopped
2 tbls frozen peas
2 tbls chopped fresh parsley
salt and pepper

To make the filling, place the onion,
garlic, chilli, chilli powder and beef
in a saucepan and fry over moderate
heat for 8 minutes, stirring.

Add the tomatoes, peas and parsley.
Season to taste and cook another 4
minutes.

Heat the sandwich maker. Spread
the butter on one side of each slice of
bread. Place 2 slices, buttered side
down, on top of the preheated cooking plate.

Spoon the filling over the slices
and top with the remaining bread
slices, buttered side up.

Close the lid and toast for 3-4
minutes.

● From top: **Croque monsieur; Cox's
cheese toastie; Scotch woodcock;
Samosa toast**

PARTY CANAPES

These are appetizers of fresh, fried or toasted bread (or biscuits) with a simple savoury, decorative topping.

Serve canapés with drinks before a meal, or at drinks parties, or as a starter to a meal.

Canapés should be about 4-5 cm (1½-2 inches) square, or similar size round, or a fancy shape made with cutters.

Cut the shapes from firm fresh bread — for example, rye bread, pumpernickel or stoneground bread for serving fresh, or medium sliced brown or white bread for toasting or frying. Cut shapes and toast, or

● From top: Eastern delights; Prawn cocktailers; Garlic gherkin; Seafood islands; Eastern delights

make the toast first and then cut into shapes.

Fry bread shapes in butter or savoury butter with a little oil added, until crisp. They can be served hot or cold depending on the topping.

Alternatively, cut larger bread rounds 6-7.5 cm (2½-3 inches) and spread butter or savoury butter on both sides. Place into patty tins and bake in the oven at 200°C, 400°F, Gas Mark 6 for about 12 minutes until crisp.

Eastern delights

MAKES 16

4 slices medium sliced white or
   brown bread, crusts removed
65 g (2½ oz) herbs and garlic butter
   (see page 13)
2 tsp vegetable oil
175 g (6 oz) finely mashed potato
1-2 tsp curry paste
To garnish
cayenne pepper
16 whole blanched almonds,
   toasted

Cut each slice of bread into 4 rounds or fancy shapes.

Melt 50 g (2 oz) of the butter and the oil in a large frying pan and fry all the bread shapes over moderate heat until crisp and golden. Drain on absorbent kitchen paper so that the fat is absorbed.

Add the remaining butter to the mashed potato with the curry paste to taste. Make sure the mixture is smooth.

Spoon the mixture into a piping bag fitted with a large star nozzle. Pipe a large whirl on to each canapé then sprinkle with cayenne pepper and garnish each with a lightly toasted almond.

Prawn cocktailers

MAKES 8

8 slices white bread
65 g (2½ oz) lemon and parsley
   butter, melted (see page 13)
2-3 lettuce leaves, finely sliced and
   chopped
75 g (3 oz) peeled prawns
2 tbls prawn cocktail sauce
paprika, for sprinkling

Heat the oven to 200°C, 400°F, Gas Mark 6. Roll the slices of bread gently with a rolling pin. Cut out 8 rounds with a 7.5 cm (3 inch) cutter. Brush the rounds with the melted butter.

Press the rounds into patty tins. Bake in the oven for 10-12 minutes until crisp. Leave to cool on a wire rack.

Place a little shredded lettuce into each bread basket with a few prawns on top.

Spoon the sauce over and sprinkle with paprika. Serve immediately.

Variation: Chopped hard-boiled egg could be used as a final topping. The leftover bread can be used for breadcrumbs.

Garlic gherkin

MAKES 16

4 slices wholemeal toast, crusts
  removed
85 g (3 oz) packet garlic and herb
  soft cheese or French roulé
  cheese
1 tbls single cream
½ red pepper, seeded and finely
  chopped (2 strips reserved)
3 mini gherkins, finely chopped
16 mini gherkins, to garnish

Cut each slice of toast into 4 squares
or rounds.

Mix the cheese and cream
together, then stir in the red pepper
and chopped gherkin. Spread the
mixture over the squares. Make fans
with the 16 gherkins and reserved
pepper. Use to garnish each canapé.

Seafood islands

MAKES 16

4 slices rye bread or pumpernickel
75 g (3 oz) full fat soft cheese
1 tbls thousand island dressing
1 tsp lemon juice
50 g (2 oz) smoked salmon,
  chopped
To garnish
16 peeled prawns
2 tsp lumpfish roe (optional)

Cut each slice of rye bread or pumpernickel into 4 squares.

Mix the cheese, dressing and lemon
juice together, stir in the salmon.

Spread the mixture on the bread
squares and garnish each with a
prawn and a little roe, if using.
Use lemon rind for an alternative
garnish.

PARTY SANDWICHES

These sandwiches are fun to prepare and make attractive eats to offer your guests. Party sandwiches are suitable for a wide range of occasions. Try asparagus slices for dainty finger eats at a reception. Open sandwiches provide more substantial food for a lunchtime or evening party while club sandwiches make an excellent savoury party sandwich at anytime.

Make these sandwiches up to three hours in advance. Cover the sandwiches with cling film, foil or a cloth and store in the refrigerator until ready to serve.

Curried club sandwich

SERVES 4

*8 slices medium sliced wheatgerm
   bread
4 slices medium sliced white bread
50 g (2 oz) butter or margarine,
   softened
4 tbls mayonnaise
1 tbls curry paste, to taste
100 g (4 oz) cooked chicken, diced
2 tsp sultanas
50 g (2 oz) low fat soft cheese
2.5 cm (1 inch) piece cucumber,
   thinly sliced
6 slices peppered salami, cut into
   strips
3 radicchio leaves, shredded
   (optional)
salt and pepper*

Trim all the slices of bread to the same size if necessary.

Butter one side of each slice of brown bread. Mix the mayonnaise with the curry paste and stir in the chicken and sultanas. Spread this mixture over 4 slices of the brown bread.

Spread the cheese over the slices of white bread. Place on top of the chicken filling. Top with the cucumber, salami and radicchio. Season if necessary. Place the remaining slices of brown bread, buttered sides down, on top.

Cut in half to serve.

Variation: Use ham or bacon instead of the salami and chopped Chinese leaves or dried, red pepper instead of the radicchio.

Asparagus slices

MAKES 10

*10 slices medium sliced
   wheatgerm bread, crusts
   removed
65 g (2½ oz) lemon and parsley
   butter (see page 13)
20-30 asparagus spears (thawed if
   frozen, drained if canned)*

Roll the slices of bread gently with a rolling pin.

Spread the bread slices with the butter and place 3 asparagus spears on each slice in a pyramid, trimming the stalks to fit. If the spears are large, place 2 on each slice of bread.

Roll the bread quite tightly round the asparagus.

Serve each roll cut into 4-5 slices.

Variation: Use half white and half brown bread and arrange the rolls alternately for serving.

Avocado and prawn

SERVES 4

*6 tbls mayonnaise
1-2 tsp tomato ketchup
4 slices wholemeal bread
1 large avocado, peeled, stoned
   and thinly sliced
2 tsp lemon juice
100 g (4 oz) peeled prawns*
To garnish
*1 slice lemon, quartered
4 sprigs parsley (optional)
red pepper strips (optional)*

Mix the mayonnaise and ketchup together. Spread all but about 2 tablespoons of this mixture on the slices of bread.

Place the avocado slices in a diagonal line on the bread. Sprinkle them with lemon juice.

Add the prawns to the remaining mayonnaise and put a spoonful either side of the line of avocado.

Garnish with lemon and with parsley sprigs and pepper strips, if using.

Variation: Use hard-boiled egg slices instead of the avocado, and rye instead of wholemeal bread.

• From top: Asparagus slices; Hawaiian chicken; Avocado and prawn; Curried club sandwich

---

Hawaiian chicken

SERVES 4

2 sesame seed baps, halved
25 g (1 oz) butter or margarine, softened
2-3 curly endive leaves or lettuce
1 large cooked chicken breast, sliced
2 pineapple rings, halved
1 fresh peach, stoned and sliced
1 tsp lemon juice
2 tbls thousand island dressing
2 tbls desiccated coconut, toasted
pepper

Spread the baps with butter and place the endive on top of each buttered half.

Arrange alternate slices of chicken, pineapple and peach over the top. Sprinkle with lemon juice and spoon the dressing down the centre. Top with coconut and pepper.

Basic quick bread

MAKES 1 × 1 KG (2 LB) TIN LOAF, 2 × 450 G (1 LB) TIN LOAVES OR 18 ROLLS

750 g (1½ lb) strong plain white flour
1 tsp salt
25 g (1 oz) lard, cut into pieces
1 sachet easi-blend dried yeast
approximately 450 ml (¾ pint) warm water

Sift the flour and salt into a large bowl. Add the lard and rub in until the mixture resembles fine crumbs.

Stir in the dried yeast. Add the water and mix to a soft, but not sticky, dough. Add a little more water if necessary.

Knead the dough on a lightly floured surface for 5 minutes.

Place the dough in a lightly oiled polybag. Leave in a warm place for 45 minutes or until it has doubled in size.

Knead the dough on a lightly floured surface for 5 minutes, then shape as required into loaves or rolls.

To shape 2 tin loaves
Divide the dough in half. Knead each piece lightly and flatten it out to the length of a 450 g (1 lb) loaf tin and 3 times the width.

Fold the dough in 3 by folding the short edges over the centre. Put each piece into a lightly oiled loaf tin. Brush the tops with lightly salted water.

Place the tins in a lightly oiled polybag. Leave in a warm place to prove for 40 minutes or until the dough reaches the top of the tins.

● Basic bread dough in various forms. Left: a cooked tin loaf; Centre: bread dough ready for shaping; Above right: a selection of rolls topped with maw (poppy) seeds; Below right: egg-glazed rolls topped with a sprinkling of buckwheat

Heat the oven to 200°C, 400°F, Gas Mark 6. Remove the polybag and glaze the loaves with salted water again, or milk.

Bake in the oven for about 35-40 minutes until golden brown and shrinking from the sides of the tin.

For a really crusty loaf, turn the bread out of the tins on to the baking sheet and continue cooking for 5-10 more minutes.

Tap the base of the loaf with your knuckles. If it sounds hollow, the bread is cooked. Leave to cool on a wire rack.

To shape 18 rolls
Divide the dough into 18 pieces.

For round dinner rolls Roll each piece of dough on a lightly floured surface. Press down on it hard with the palm of your hand, making circling movements and gradually cupping the palm of your hand round the dough to form a smooth ball.

For knotty rolls Roll each piece of dough into a thin rope, about 25 cm (10 inches) long, and tie it in a plump, loose knot. (See picture.)

For cottage rolls Divide each piece of dough into 3. Knead 2 of the pieces together and form into a ball. Knead the remaining piece of dough into a small ball, brush with water and place on top of the larger ball. Flour your finger and push it right through the top to the centre to stick the 2 balls of dough together.

For clover rolls Divide each piece of dough into 3 and shape into 3 small balls. Place them just touching on a baking sheet.

For 'S' shapes Roll each piece of dough into a thick sausage and shape it into an 'S'.

Put the rolls, spaced apart, on lightly oiled baking sheets. Cover with oiled cling film or polybag. Leave to prove for about 20-30 minutes or until doubled in size.

Heat the oven to 230°C, 450°F, Gas Mark 8.

Remove the cling film and brush with salted water or milk to glaze. Sprinkle with poppy/maw seeds, sesame seeds or buckwheat, if liked.

Bake in the oven for about 10-15 minutes or until golden brown. Leave to cool on a wire rack.

Enriched bread dough

MAKES 1 LARGE PLAIT OR 18 ROLLS

750 g (1½ lb) strong plain white
flour
1 tsp salt
1 sachet easi-blend dried yeast
50 g (2 oz) butter, melted
375-450 ml (13-15 fl oz) milk,
warmed
1 egg, beaten
1 tsp caster sugar

Sift the flour and salt into a large bowl and stir in the yeast.

Add the butter and milk and all but 1 tablespoon of the egg. Reserve for glazing. Mix the ingredients to a soft dough. Knead the dough on a lightly floured surface for 5 minutes.

Place the dough in a lightly oiled polybag and leave in a warm place for 45 minutes or until it has doubled in size.

Knead the dough on a lightly floured surface for 5 minutes, then shape as required into 1 large or 2 small plaits or several rolls.

To shape a plait

Divide the dough into 3 and roll each piece into a 30 cm (12 inch) long sausage.

Lay the 3 sausages side by side on a flat surface. Join them at one end and plait them by passing the left piece over the centre one, then the right piece over the centre one and so on, until the length is plaited. Join the short ends neatly together and tuck them under the plait.

Place the plait on a lightly greased baking sheet. Beat the reserved egg with 1 tsp caster sugar and 1 tbls water to make a glaze. Brush the glaze evenly over the plait and sprinkle with seeds, if wished.

Put the baking sheet inside a lightly oiled polybag. Leave in a warm place to prove until the dough has doubled in size.

Heat the oven to 190°C, 375°F, Gas Mark 5.

Remove the polybag. Bake in the oven for 35-40 minutes. Tap the base of the loaf with your knuckles; if it sounds hollow, the bread is cooked. Leave to cool on a wire rack.

Granary bread

MAKES 2 × 1 KG (2 LB) LOAVES

1.25 kg (3 lb) malted granary flour
2 tsp salt
2 sachets easi-blend dried yeast
1 tsp brown sugar or black treacle
900 ml (1½ pints) warm water
beaten egg, to glaze
little buckwheat, for sprinkling
(optional)

Mix the flour, salt and yeast in a large warmed bowl.

Add the sugar or treacle to the water and stir into the flour to make a soft pliable dough.

Knead the dough by hand on a lightly floured surface for 10 minutes, or in an electric mixer with a dough hook for 5 minutes, until the dough is smooth and elastic.

Place the dough in the bowl and cover with lightly oiled cling film, or polybag. Leave in a warm place for 1 hour or until it has doubled in size.

Turn the dough on to a lightly floured surface and cut in half. Knead each piece until smooth, then place in 2 × 1 kg (2 lb) loaf tins.

Place the tins in a large, lightly oiled polybag and tie loosely. Leave in a warm place to prove for about 30 minutes or until the dough rises above the sides of the tin.

Heat the oven to 220°C, 425°F, Gas Mark 7. Remove the polybag. Brush loaves with beaten egg and sprinkle with buckwheat if using.

Bake in the oven for 30-45 minutes. Tap the base of the loaves with your knuckles; if it sounds hollow, the bread is cooked. Leave to cool on a wire rack.

Variation: The bread can be shaped into rounds and cooked on greased, floured baking sheets. The top can be glazed with salted water.

● Back row: Granary dough and tin loaf; Front: Enriched bread dough plait, and dinner rolls (see instructions on page 59)

Brioche

MAKES 18

350 g (12 oz) plain flour
good pinch of salt
1 tsp caster sugar
150 g (5 oz) butter, softened
1 sachet easi-blend dried yeast
2 eggs, beaten
3 tbls milk, warmed
beaten egg, to glaze
poppy or sesame seeds, for
  sprinkling (optional)

Sift the flour into a large bowl. Add the salt and sugar, then rub in the butter.

Stir in the yeast. Beat the eggs and milk together. Add to the bowl and mix to a soft dough. Knead the dough on a work surface (you should not need to use flour) for about 5 minutes until smooth.

Place the dough in the bowl and cover with lightly oiled cling film or a polybag. Leave in a warm place for about 1 hour or until it has doubled in size. Do not put the dough in too hot a place or the butter will melt and spoil the dough texture.

Turn the dough on to the work surface and cut into 18 pieces.

Cut a quarter off each piece of dough and roll each portion into a ball. Place the smaller ball on top of the larger one and press it down firmly into the dough with your finger.

Place the brioche in well greased individual brioche moulds or deep bun tins. Cover with lightly oiled cling film or a polybag. Leave for about 40 minutes or until it has doubled in size.

Heat the oven to 220°C, 425°F, Gas Mark 7. Brush the brioche with beaten egg, then sprinkle with poppy or sesame seeds, if using.

Bake in the oven for 10 minutes until golden. Remove from the tins. Leave to cool on a wire rack.

Serving idea: Serve warm with butter, preserves and honey for breakfast, or with savoury (cheese, ham and egg) or sweet (fruit and cream) fillings for tea.

Variation: Make one large brioche in a 20 cm (8 inch) tin and bake for 30 minutes.

Wheaty soda bread

MAKES 1 LOAF

225 g (8 oz) 100% wholewheat flour
225 g (8 oz) plain flour
½ tsp salt
1 tsp bicarbonate of soda
50 g (2 oz) butter or block
* margarine*
150 g (5.29 oz) carton natural
* yoghurt*
150 ml (¼ pint) milk
wholewheat flour, for dusting

Heat the oven to 200°C, 400°F, Gas Mark 6. Sift the flours, salt and bicarbonate of soda into a large bowl. Tip back into the bowl any bran left in the sieve.

Rub in the butter until the mixture resembles fine breadcrumbs. Stir in the yoghurt and enough milk to make a fairly stiff dough. Try not to handle the dough too much or be tempted to add too much milk or the dough will be heavy and close-textured.

Shape the dough into a large ball, place on a greased baking sheet and flatten the ball slightly. Score the top diagonally with a sharp knife, then sprinkle with flour.

Bake in the oven for 30 minutes or until the loaf sounds hollow when tapped on the base with your knuckles. Leave to cool on a wire rack.

Variation: Flavour the dough by adding herbs or Parmesan cheese to the mixture before adding the liquid.

● Left: Brioche dough proving in a bowl, brioche rolls proven and shaped, and cooked brioche rolls in the foreground; Right: A cooked loaf of wheaty soda bread and in the background the dough shaped and ready for baking

INDEX